# Self Esteem Workbook

*Gain Self-Esteem & Confidence, Healing Through Self Love and Affirmations for Women, Men and Teens*

# TABLE OF CONTENTS

# INTRODUCTION

Our happiness and overall mental health are tied to a great extent on our thoughts. There is no way you can live a happy and fulfilling life if you think of yourself as a scumbag, good-for-nothing, ugly, inefficient, dull and useless fellow. It takes believing you are worthy, deserving and capable of achieving greatness to pursue a lifestyle of greatness.

You tend to behave in ways that will have you feeling worse about yourself and depressed about your life when you have low self-esteem. And when your mental or physical health is poor, your dreams and potentials suffer for it.

Although it may seem impossible –like there is no changing the way you see yourself and how you feel about yourself, building a healthy self-esteem is attainable. This book will show you, in the simplest way, how you can silence the criticizing voice, learn to accept and love yourself, stop worrying about what others think of you and raise your sense of self-worth.

In case you haven't noticed, nearly everything that makes people happy –marriage, raising a family, a great job, self-respect and so on—requires work. Self-esteem is like that too, it also requires a bit of your time and effort. So, get ready to do more than just reading this book and feeling good about yourself for a couple of days.

To become the confident person you've always wanted to be, you have to read, practice and keep practicing—consistency will get you there!

# CHAPTER 1
## UNDERSTANDING SELF-ESTEEM

People who have no self-esteem often think that they will become confident and happy with themselves when their current situation changes. Seeing a beautiful face when you look into the mirror will make you walk with your shoulders high up, having caring parents will make you feel normal and happy, scoring all A's in your exam will enable you look your classmates in the eye and say whatever you want, your neighbors will respect you when you own a car and that will boost your confidence, getting married will elevate your status and in turn, make you feel less inferior about yourself.

Self-esteem or the lack thereof, is related to external circumstances. "If A or B happens, my self-esteem will increase," so they think. While it is possible that you will see yourself in a better light and get a sense of self-worth from achieving great things, that level of highness you feel will most likely not last. Why? Self-esteem is basically a state of mind. Although, the current state of your life and other people's opinion of you may have a bearing on your self-esteem, the ultimate determinant of your self-esteem is your thoughts.

Take this scenario for instance, Unemployed Miss A thinks Miss B who is employed is more intelligent and better than she is. Employed Miss B tells herself that she would have been running her own business by now if only she was as smart and efficient as her entrepreneur friend. Then there is Miss C who is also unemployed but thinks her situation is not as a result of her not being good enough but because she is yet to develop the skills needed for the job.

What differentiates Miss C from both Miss A and Miss B? The way she sees herself. Miss C understands that she doesn't possess the skills that will land her the job she wants but instead of thinking there is something inherently wrong with her, she singles out the problem and separates it from her core being.

Between Miss C and Miss B, who do you think lives a happy life? It's Miss C of course. As humans, we are aware of our identity: hating the way we look, how we act or the family we come from automatically cripples our sense of self-worth. Your level of self-esteem usually depends on how much you like and appreciate yourself.

Don't confuse healthy self-esteem with too high or 'overly inflated' self-esteem though. Thinking you are superior to everybody is just as psychologically unhealthy as seeing yourself as the dust of the earth—the worst being on earth, underserving of love. You overestimate your abilities, praise yourself too much and expect others to do the same even when you don't deserve it. Other people are seen through a diminishing lens and you act as though the world revolves around you.

Having self-esteem that is too high is dangerous and damaging, especially because it prevents you from embracing self-improvement.

The next segment of this book examines the dimensions of self-esteem further, your aim should be to have a moderate self-esteem.

## The Problem with Self-esteem

Self-esteem is more complicated than the popular 'high vs low' concept that is often used to describe it. If you say you have a high self-esteem, does it mean you never have moments of self-doubt? And for those who think they have a low self-esteem, has there never been a time you felt proud or good about yourself? It can be hard to know for sure what your level of self-esteem is, because feelings fluctuate. One minute you feel so good about yourself and the next minute you are plagued with self-doubt.

Being the human that you are, it is normal to experience varying feelings—both positive and negative. In order to fully benefit from this book, measuring your self-esteem by taking the following self-esteem checkup will be extremely helpful. Be honest as you can when answering the questions. The answers you give will help you recognize how you esteem yourself.

The Self-Esteem Checkup

To avoid complicating things, this book will be using the words 'healthy 'and 'poor' to describe the positive and negative angles of self-esteem. Self-esteem that is too high or overly inflated is not healthy, but you can't call it low either. Poor self-esteem better incorporates both low and too high self-esteem. To know the dimension of self-esteem that best describes you, do the exercise below.

Which of the following statements do you believe to be true or false about yourself? Rate from 0 to 10, with 10 meaning you completely believe it to be true and 0 meaning you don't believe it at all (Schiraldi 1999).

| **Statement** | **Rating** |
|---|---|
| 1.  I like the face I see in the mirror | _____________ |
| 2.  I'd rather be me than someone else | _____________ |
| 3.  I feel like a colossal failure | _____________ |
| 4.  I respect myself | _____________ |
| 5.  Even when others reject me, I still like myself | _____________ |
| 6.  I am satisfied with the kind of person I'm becoming | _____________ |
| 7.  I can laugh at myself | _____________ |
| 8.  I am more valuable than any other person | _____________ |
| 9.  I believe I am capable of achieving greatness | _____________ |
| 10. I love and support myself, regardless of external circumstances | _____________ |
| Total Score | _____________ |

Now that you are done with that, rate on a scale of 1 to 5, how often the above thought-patterns limit your lifestyle or affect your daily activities? And how severe your struggle with self-esteem is.

## How Self-esteem Develops

Everybody has a measure of self-esteem and the level of self-esteem you have now has a source. Our childhood, that innocent period when we didn't know our left from our right, when we were led by the hands and guided by our parents and other grown-ups in our lives, is usually a major decisive factor of our self-esteem.

You didn't know that touching fire could burn the skin until your parents told you. Talking loudly, eating while you talk, sitting with your legs spread wide in a panties-revealing way as a girl, not combing your hair, not brushing your teeth every morning, mingling with your unruly neighbors, collecting something from a stranger or running around in the streets are some behaviors your parents probably told you to desist from doing.

Parents who model self-esteem know how to get their kids to do the right thing while also respecting the individuality and opinions of their children. They encourage you, consistently show you love, back you up when necessary and make you understand in a clear and reasonable way, how they expect you to behave. These types of parents make sure it sinks in that it is your behavior that is bad, not you as a human being.

Authoritarian parents or permissive parents on the other hand, usually have a poor way of using words as they tend to be less concerned about the feelings or mental growth of their children. "Stop littering the floor, dirty child," they say or "bad child, you can never do anything right." Each inappropriate behavior you display earns you doses of scolding or spanking. Some parents even go to the extent of pushing their kids away or denying them of something essential to their existence like food or school fees when their children misbehaves.

Consciously or unconsciously, you know that your survival depends on your parents as a child. Their approval matters a lot to you as you don't want to lose their support. Automatically, you start thinking of yourself as a bad, useless or lazy person when you find yourself staying till nightfall without brushing your teeth, hanging out with your 'unruly' neighbors, talking loudly or doing some other thing that you often receive punishment for doing.

All of these feelings seep into your teenage and adulthood, inflicting your self-esteem. You will find yourself constantly struggling to unlearn what you were often told was the best way to behave or the standard form of beauty. As a grown up, you've probably discovered that beauty is not tied to a single physical appearance, there are different forms of beauty. But when you look in the mirror, you can't help thinking you are ugly because your nose is flat, your forehead is wide, and your skin is dark.

And it all reverts back to thoughts, no matter where your self-esteem stems from: parents, traumatic experience or negative peers, one major factor binds all your feelings and your sense of self-worth together: your thoughts. You should put effort towards challenging your debasing, embarrassing or painful thoughts.

Although, when a child is always told that he or she is ugly, lazy, and stingy or dull, he or she grows up with a nagging sense of wrongness. It becomes hard work to be convinced otherwise. Fortunately, building healthy self-esteem can only be difficult not impossible. As earlier stated, the key to becoming the confident person you desire to be is to consistently use the tools and practice the tips contained in this book.

## Why Healthy Self-esteem is Important

Why should you invest your time and effort into increasing your self-esteem? Your overall health and performance depends on it. When you judge and reject yourself, you bring pain upon yourself. Life becomes unexciting and you engage in activities that are harmful to your health. It is not uncommon to find people struggling with their self-esteem abusing alcohol and drugs, eating poorly, becoming promiscuous, enduring abusive relationships or suffering from psychosomatic illnesses like indigestion, headache, fatigue and insomnia.

As you think that people will hate you or not want to associate with you, you withdraw from social settings and end up feeling lonely. Anxiety, stress symptoms and depression are usually the accompanying baggage of poor self-esteem. Your performance at school and work also bears the brunt of your self-esteem. In the absence of healthy self-esteem, fear overshadows the drive to seize and maximize opportunities for growth.

The fear of self-rejection and judgment makes you take less academic, career or social risks. You already believe that you won't succeed, not when people who are better than you are around, so you shy away from job interviews or meeting people.

Living with a negative sense of self-worth prevents you from maximizing your full potential as it limits your ability ask for help, handle criticism, express yourself and solve problems. It's like being your own prisoner, you have an idea that you are capable of achieving so much more but since you are locked behind the gate of unbelief and fear, you remain stagnant.

With a healthy self-esteem comes the ability to navigate life with an assertive and positive attitude –to be truly free from the cage of perfectionism, poor perception of self and self-rejection. You can stop the judgments and change the way you feel about yourself. The next chapter is about challenging your thoughts and actively fighting back the judgmental voice.

# CHAPTER 2
# THE VICIOUS INNER CRITIC

The vicious inner critic is that voice you hear in your every waking moment, it is part of your thoughts. Always with you, pointing out reasons, in the most vicious way possible, why you shouldn't go to that party, meet new people, bother about eating right, go on that date, prepare for that presentation and so on. You are a big-headed and dull-looking fellow that nobody is interested in knowing, it tells you, what will your date like about you or why would people want to hear what you have to say?

On and on it goes, reading people's minds and firing their supposed opinions at you which you believe to be true. Everyone has a critical inner voice, but it is more vicious and vocal with those whose self-esteem is poor. Eugene Sagan, a psychologist, refers to this voice as a 'pathological critic.' Everything this pathological critic has to say is usually negative, full of judgments that attack your core being.

You may not even notice the damaging effects this voice has on you because the inner voice seems natural, like a part of you. You are directly aware of yourself and the world around you, it's easy to think that the critic's judgments are normal and true. Deep down, you think you are worthless and a waste of space so when the inner critic repeats those words to you, you don't find it strange or feel a need to defend yourself.

But that's not normal at all! You shouldn't notice what you feel and do through the eyes of the inner critic. The critic usually exaggerates and distorts reality. Out of the one hour you spent with your first date, the critic pans down on the single mistake you made, concluding that you were such a boring and nervous wreck and that your date won't be interested in seeing you again. Even if you acted normal and reasonable, the critic still finds a way to blow things out of proportion and make you feel bad about yourself.

The critic makes you feel transparent –like people can see through you and will definitely be turned off by what they see. Sometimes, all it takes for the critic to switch off your good mood and suppress you with feelings of disgust is simply one word: incompetent, lazy, screw-up, ugly, weirdo, dull and so on.

If you focus and pay attention to your thoughts when you are feeling anxious or depressed, you may notice that the voice sounds familiar. The critical remarks are in your mother's voice or your father's or even in your own voice.

When was the first time your inner critic showed up? Most likely after the first two or three years of your life, when you were being handed the rules to live by. These rules could be clear, vague or inconsistent. The forbidding, disapproving or punishing voice that shaped your behavior as a child arises again and again when you make a mistake, incite somebody's anger or fall short of a goal.

The critic is often quick and happy to bring up memories from your past, taunting you with embarrassing scenes that proves you can't do it any different this time around. But that's just one of the tools that this domineering critic uses to judge and attack your self-worth. Being aware of where the critic originated from and the weapons it uses to control you are steps towards fighting back the vicious inner critic.

## Rules, comparison and perfectionism

These are the three major weapons of the inner critic. It sets such high standards for you and as you almost never attain them, you end up feeling useless. You love music and want to be a musician but regardless of how talented and successful you are in that field, you never feel good enough because the critic tells you that you can only be acceptable or respected as a lawyer.

Your parents are probably not in support of you doing anything other than studying law and even though you rebelled, dropped out and pursued your dreams anyway, self-doubt sleeps next to you nearly every night. The critic keeps using self-statements that align with your parent's views and it works every single time.

Comparison is just as effective. The critic is fond of pairing you next to others and evaluating you in terms of sexual attractiveness, intelligence, likability, social competence, earning capacity and virtually any traits you desire for yourself. You feel less adequate when the critic tells you that you don't measure up to others.

The critic constantly makes you feel bad for not being perfect. Perfectionism: you are either great at communicating or totally bad at it, a top performer at work or a loser. You have to graduate with 5.0 or you're dull and less than your siblings who graduated with that grade. You have to be earning seven figures or are a lousy breadwinner who shouldn't sit on the same table with his mates who make that amount of money. And you listen to the critic.

## Why you listen to and believe the inner critic

You do so because it helps you solve your basic needs. Insecurity, fear, incompetence, ostracization and worthlessness are feelings that no one likes experiencing. While your inner critic screams words that denies you of your basic needs, it ironically provides you with a solution that gives you a sense of being okay. Despite the devastating effects of listening to the vicious voice of your inner critic, you begin to rely on it to cope with feelings of anxiety and depression.

You want to feel close to and be accepted by your parents, so you listen to your critic when it attacks you for being immoral or a failure in the exact same tones your parents use. It's easy to believe the critic because you believed your parents. Seeing things through the eyes of your parents also makes you feel close to them and more accepted.

You may think of yourself as adequate when you compare yourself to others you find less attractive or intelligent than you are. Relieving the few moments you felt better about yourself helps you cope with meeting others you think are better than you.

The rare periods of time you attain the high standards that your critic sets for you makes you feel good, so you keep insisting on being perfect.

You fear failure and that makes you anxious, when you try to take actions that will elevate your status, your critic discourages you by telling you will fail. You decide not to do anything and immediately feel less anxious.

By listening to the critic and not making substantial efforts to do that which could increase your self-worth, you don't feel much pain when your fears materialize because the critic already prepared you for that. If you fear rejection, the critic tells you in clear and loud terms that you won't be accepted and you reject yourself first, so being rejected by others doesn't hurt so much.

This coping mechanism is bad because while it helps you, it further undermines your self-worth at the same time.

There are better ways to meet your basic needs, approaches you can follow. But first, you need to monitor and catch your inner vicious critic. Start taking note of your inner monologues and the needs they help you solve. It is highly important that you practice the next step.

## Monitoring and Silencing the Critic

Since the critic feels natural as it is woven into your thoughts, you have to carefully and constantly monitor your thoughts in order to catch it red-handed. Doing these two exercises outlined below will help you stay alert to the self-attacks and critical statements your critics shoot at you.

**Exercise 1:**

Get a notebook and draw three lines on a page. In the first column, number your thoughts. Write down the critical statements in the second column and in the last column, note down the time you had those thoughts. Taking note of the time will help you know how frequent and how often you have these thoughts.

Your note would look something like this

| Number | Critical Statement | Time |
| --- | --- | --- |
| 1 | Scattered room. God! I'm so disorganized and dirty | 5:00PM |
| 2 | Why am I so abnormal and weird? Nobody even wants to be my friend | 5:55PM |

**Exercise 2:**

In the same notebook, draw another three lines. Represent the critical statement in the previous table with a number in the first column. In the second column, write down what the thought helps you avoid and in the third column, how it helps you feel or act.

Here is an example:

| Thought number | Helps you avoid | Helps you feel or act |
| --- | --- | --- |
| 1 | | Motivated to remember arranging and cleaning your room |
| 2 | Feeling less anxious. I already know I'm awkward and abnormal, so they can't hurt me. | |

Once you start monitoring the critic, you will notice a pattern to the way it works. The critic tends to overgeneralize, filter reality, use labels, blame you for everything, read minds and personalize every single thing. To silence the critic, you have to create a rebuttal voice that will talk back in a specific, clear and loud manner. Strange, though it may seem, talking back at the critic can render it useless when done the right way.

It is highly advisable to imagine your rebuttal voice as a person who will always have your back and be ever ready to fight the pathological critic on your behalf. Think of this person as an accepting friend who understands you, a healthy coach whose aim is to see you succeed, a rational teacher who is insightful and kind or a compassionate mentor who is older than you are and who you can be totally safe with.

When you talk back at your critic, let whoever you imagine the second person to be address you in the second person, saying your name and talking to you in a specific and forceful manner that's in tandem with the critic's voice. Make sure the rebuttals are balanced, based on reality while being non-judgmental at the same time.

To make it easier for you to believe these positive self-talks and fully neutralize your vicious inner critic, it helps for you to reassess yourself and initiate an alternative strategy of meeting the basic needs you crave: self-acceptance, love, security and self-worth. The next chapter gives you a framework for accurately reassessing the way you see yourself and understanding your intrinsic worth.

# CHAPTER 3
## REASSESSING YOURSELF

Your inner critic has been with you for nearly all the years of your life. Listening to and believing its voice has become a habit for you and habits are hard to break. Although, actively exchanging words with your critic is important, it won't be completely effective in silencing the critic because believing those positive words you say about yourself can be difficult.

In order to shut down the critic forever, you will have to reassess yourself and become positively aware of your core worth.

## Understanding your core worth

"We are all basically the same human beings, who seek happiness and try to avoid suffering. Everybody is my peer group. Your feeling "I am of no value" is wrong. Absolutely wrong." (The Dalai Lama)

Your core worth is independent of external factors. You are already complete! It is the idea that you can only be worthy when you are 'completed' that makes you feel bad about yourself. The critic makes you believe that your achievements, behavior or appearance are valuable droplets that will fill up the empty vessel that's your being. But that's not true, as a breathing human, your life has value.

Why do you think people are driven to save a one-year old baby who fell inside a well? He/she hasn't achieved anything in life and yet, people go through great extent to save her life. It is because we are born complete: lovable and full of potential.

A human's worth doesn't lie in what he/she has done, but on their ability to experience and perceive. Regardless of our appearance or situation, we all possess the capacity to feel various emotions, beautify life, think rationally, and correct our course when we make a mistake, or recognize truth.

When you condemn your core worth, you will always judge yourself unreasonably – feeling bad or ashamed of your core self rather than your behavior or events.

Learn to judge behavior, rather than your core. Separating your core from externals will make it easier for you to believe your positive affirmations and take actions that will benefit your life.

## A Healthy Replacement

Trying to replace the critic with positive affirmations of your worth without applying an alternative strategy that will help you meet the basic needs you relied on the critic for will have the critic returning in a short while. The following are healthier ways of meeting your need to achieve, feel/do right and avoid negative feelings:

## 1. Re-evaluate your values

The norm for you has become to rely on the critic to push you into doing the right thing, feeling better about yourself or achieving more. To release yourself from that unhealthy hold, you have to reevaluate your values. Are your goals appropriate for you? What really, is the major reason why you want what you want? Do you want it for yourself or for your parent or spouse? Answering these questions while exploring the long and short-term consequences of your answers will help you determine whether your desires are reasonable or right for you.

It will also help you discover and focus on living according to your values. The need to stick to your values will now become your motivation to do right or achieve more. You will no longer rely on the critic for motivation.

## 2. Find new motivators

Apparently, there is a need to find new motivators. The punches your critic rain down on you when you fail to work hard towards reaching your goals shouldn't be your motivational force. Replace that motivation by visualizing the approval of true friends and the benefits of achieving your goals.

## 3. Redefine your perception

You want to pursue a goal but you fear failure, so when your critic tells you not to bother, that you are not capable anyway, you don't make any effort and your fear subsides. Instead of controlling your fear of failure that way, you could change the way you view mistakes. Remember failing at something doesn't mean there is something wrong with you, all you probably need to succeed is to simply gain more experience and develop new skills.

4. Develop new skills

Rather than trying to desensitize the pain of rejection by reading people's mind and making predictions, you should focus on developing skills that will enable you speak more assertively, communicate effectively and handle criticisms better. Learning to say exactly what is on your mind will prevent you from experiencing negative feelings of anger, frustration or guilt.

5. Practice reaffirmation of your worth

When you catch yourself making comparisons in a bid to find someone who is less than you are—someone who will make you feel temporarily good about yourself, practice reaffirming your worth. Separate your core worth from externals and remember that you are intrinsically valuable. Challenge the old belief that your worth depends on your behavior or appearance. The next subheading "Cultivating Self-appreciation" will teach you how to truly love and accept who you are.

## Cultivating Self-appreciation

You can only generate affirmations that will be effective in silencing your critic when you believe that those affirmations are true. Accurately reassessing yourself is one of the best ways to cultivate self-appreciation. How real are your perceived flaws and why do you focus so much on them?

Janet was hanging out at a party with a group of friends she's always thought were better than she is in everything. Suddenly a guy walks up to the group and singles her out, trying to make conversation. Janet is surprised and bluntly asks the guy what he wants with her. The guy says he is interested in knowing more about her. Janet finds that hard to believe, "why me out of all my friends?" she asks. The guy tells her he finds her attractive. Thinking that someone was playing a cruel joke on her, Janet immediately points out her flaws "I am fat, my face is covered in pimples and I have a crooked front teeth."

The guy stops in his stride. "What were you saying again?" Janet asks. The guy says he needs to use the toilet and disappears. Now Janet will go home thinking of course, that's just the way it has always been, nobody can love her because she's so ugly. Meanwhile, the guy saw an attractive girl when he looked at her.

Everyone has specific strengths and weaknesses but people with poor self-esteem usually filter those strengths and magnify their weaknesses. The problem is not having faults you will like to change, the problem is attacking yourself with those faults. Carry out a research and you will find that nearly everyone has a thing or two they will like to change about themselves.

You experience feelings of inadequacy when you see others more accurately than you see yourself. You need to trash the distorted mirror through which you see yourself and learn to realistically balance your strengths and weaknesses. Practicing the exercise in this segment will help you recognize and value who you really are.

## A Realistic Self-description

Get your self-esteem assignment notebook again. What you will be doing this time is divided in four parts: describing the way you see every angle of your life, separating your weaknesses from your strengths, rewriting how you see your weakness and celebrating your strengths.

## Describing the way you see yourself

Don't leave anything out. Write down everything you think about your personality, physical appearance, relationships, school or work performance, other people's perception of you, sexuality and mental functioning. You could draw a table again and put each areas of your life in columns.

Be very specific when describing the way you see yourself. Use the exact words you usually describe yourself with. Every positive and negative traits you think you have –your every strength and weaknesses should be well outlined. If you think you have an ugly nose, long dark hair, beautiful smile, flat chest, put it down.

Do you consider your relationship with others to be awkward, entertaining, warm or inexistent? And others' perception of you as competent, dull, lazy or efficient? Write everything down. It is very important that you don't leave out any aspect of your life.

## Separating your weaknesses from your strengths

When you are done taking inventory of yourself, go back and put a minus sign beside every description you view as a weakness and use a plus sign to represent your strengths. You may discover that the plus and minus signs are evenly spread out in each category, meaning your strengths and weaknesses are balanced. If you have more minus than you have plus signs, you may have a harder time believing the positive affirmations you tell yourself. But not to worry though, rewriting your weaknesses can help you stop attacking yourself with those negative self-evaluations.

## Rewriting your weaknesses

As earlier stated, having faults is not the problem, it is attacking your core worth with those faults that is a big problem. Saying you are "too fat" will make you feel bad about yourself but when you say you weigh 250 pounds and will like to lose 50 pounds, your realistic evaluation of yourself will keep the feelings of depression at bay.

Rewriting your weakness involves changing your use of language. Exaggerating, pejorative and generalizing words should be absent from your vocabulary.

From your list of weaknesses, pick out words that magnify the negative like *fat tummy, total screw-up, illogical, flat chested, forgetful and so on.* You will revise those words, focusing on pure facts. Fat tummy becomes 34-inch waist for instance while forgetful is replaced with an outline of the specific things you tend to forget like names or dates.

Stop using insulting words like *ugly, lousy, dull, good-for-nothing, stupid or talkative* to describe yourself. Used sparsely, these negative words are not very dangerous but when used often, they tear your self-esteem to shreds.

Also eliminate generalizing like words *always, never, everything, everybody, completely* and so on. Reflect on the specific occasions when you behaved in a certain way instead or take note of the specific people who you act or feel a certain way with. Noting that you occasionally lose your car keys or earrings is not damaging to your worth as thinking that you lose everything. Being specific in the way you describe your weaknesses makes them less global and threatening.

## Celebrating your strengths

Learn to acknowledge your strengths and allow them to speak for you. Don't water down your strengths by coming up with reasons why they are not that good enough. Blowing your own trumpet or giving yourself credit makes you feel anxious or bad probably because your critical parents always found a way to make you feel you could have done much better as a child.

Stop listening to the critic, silence it by affirming your true strengths. If you find it hard to pinpoint your strengths, try remembering your little successes, the prizes or awards you've earned, compliments you've received and any single thing you value about yourself.

It may also help to list out the qualities you like about those you love and admire. Examine yourself accurately to see if you possess similar qualities. You may be surprised to find that you are not so different from them.

To start believing your realistic self-description, you have to write a new description of yourself that you will read out to yourself every day for a month till it drowns out the voice of the vicious inner critic that you've been listening to for years. The new description should incorporate the tips outlined above: no use of pejoratives, generalization, exaggeration or vagueness.

Make sure you defend yourself with positive affirmations of your strength whenever your critic starts bombarding you with negativity. Let the rebuttal voice of your accepting friend, rational teacher, healthy coach or compassionate mentor do the talking. Sure, the critic can be cunny and relentless, attacking you with memories or thoughts that are hard for you to ignore, making your attempts at accurate thinking useless.

But you can still emerge a victor in this war against the critic. Distancing yourself from your mind or thoughts is another weapon you can add to the special arsenal you have for fighting the critic. You will learn how to do that in the next chapter.

# CHAPTER 4
## HOW TO STOP BEING SELF-ABSORBED

People with poor self-esteem are usually too self-absorbed or too conscious of themselves. And that's because they think people are always paying attention to the way they look, talk, walk or act. When you are in a social setting, your thoughts are tuned inwards. It revolves around you, you, you and what everyone sees when they look at you—usually not anything positive.

Instead of having a great time, you are busy thinking about what other people are thinking. Due to the fact that you are present in that situation, watching people's faces and attempting to read their minds, silencing the critic with your positive affirmation can be difficult.

The tormenting thoughts keep flooding your mind. You seek approving looks and words from others, forgetting that it is what you think about yourself already that counts. If you already think you are ugly and you hear someone say that about you, you will immediately believe that you are because the person is only confirming your thoughts. However, if you see yourself as an intelligent being and someone accuses you of being dull, your reaction to those will be shock or disbelief rather than acceptance.

While receiving great compliments and being loved by others is a good self-esteem booster, it is not the bedrock of self-esteem. Why? No one can damage your self-esteem without your consent. A major step to becoming less self-conscious even with the barrage of those torturing thoughts, is to detach yourself from your mind.

## Ignoring your present thoughts

Not all your thoughts are important or true. You can learn to only observe your thoughts without paying attention to them. The trick is to start seeing your thoughts as just that 'thoughts', not you or part of you— fleeting thoughts that you can just watch till they drift away.

When next you are feeling down or bad about yourself, try separating your thoughts from your core being by noticing that you are merely *having a thought that you are incompetent* and not that *you are incompetent*. It is just a thought!

The two major tools that you can use to distance yourself from your thoughts are meditation and thought labeling.

## Meditation

You can make your thoughts incapable of overwhelming you by simply focusing on your breath and watching them. Start by staying still and imagining that your thoughts are flies entering through the window of your house and buzzing across the room. Notice each one of them, allow them fly without analyzing them or getting attached to them. Do it with every single thought, no matter how persistent or urgent they are—simply observe each one of them till the next one comes along.

While you acknowledge each thought as they come, focus on breathing. It is best to keep count of your breaths so that you will always go back to them after you have acknowledged any thought that showed up.

As you observe your thoughts, you may notice that they are slowing down and that you are beginning to feel calmer. Regardless of how you feel though while meditating, it is important that you learn to watch your thoughts.

## Thought labeling

Labeling your thoughts is another way to detach yourself from them. Whenever the critic starts screaming that you are unlovable or a good-for-nothing, repeat the thought you are having by phrasing them this way: "I'm having a thought that I am unlovable or good for nothing." Once you label the thoughts this way, they will instantly become less pressing and believable.

It also helps to notice and describe the kind of thought you are having. For instance, you could say "my mind is having judgment thoughts, embarrassing thoughts, mistake thoughts or fear thoughts. You become a mere observer, noticing your thoughts without being your thoughts.

To further distance yourself from those judgment or fear thoughts, you can also thank your mind for generating those thoughts. You say "thank you, mind, for that fear thought." This distances the thought from your cognition.

## Letting go of painful/embarrassing memories or thoughts

The critic is very good at replaying scenes from your past that you find painful or embarrassing. It never forgets the names of people that hurt you in the past or occasions when you did something that made you feel like sinking into the ground with shame. When the critic attacks you with thoughts like this, simply observing and ignoring those thoughts can be very difficult.

Even though you see a beautiful face when you look into the mirror now, walking down the streets, thoughts of the times when you were too thin, pimple-faced and flat-chested cloud your mind. If you were taunted for the way you look, that is all you hear when you meet other people. It can be really hard to challenge or ignore your thoughts because the derogative words are so loud in your mind and the pictures are so clear—they were once your reality for a very long time.

How do you let go of such painful/embarrassing memories or thoughts? By practicing the two steps outlined below:

## Acceptance

How about coming to accept and appreciate your past and present, so that having such thoughts won't have the power to hurt you anymore? Stop rejecting yourself for the way you looked or acted in the past. Learn to truly embrace the fact that the external world doesn't add to or take away the worthiness of your core being and that you only acted the way you did because of your level of experience at the time. Stop beating up yourself over what you cannot change.

Accept that you are not perfect. It is your desire to be perfect that makes you conscious of yourself, worrying about what others are thinking of you.

## Forgiveness

The next crucial step you should practice after acceptance is forgiveness. Learning to love yourself regardless of what you think about yourself or your past memories. You can't move on from the past if you keep regretting your actions and rejecting yourself. Practicing the following 'nevertheless' technique can help you make peace with your past.

## Exercise

Select events or memories that are capable of eroding your self-esteem and respond with a 'nevertheless' statement. For instance, when your inner critic tells you that you can never amount to much, respond with "I am not perfect, nevertheless I am growing."

Take your self-esteem assignment notebook and write on a fresh sheet, a list of three or more events or memories that always bring you down as you find them embarrassing and hurtful. Fully describe each of the memories or events and the emotional effect they have on you. Then create a perfect 'nevertheless' response to each of those statements.

# CHAPTER 5
## BEING SELF-AWARE

Quite ironic, right? The previous chapter teaches you how not to be self-conscious and this chapter is about being self-aware. Well, ignoring your thoughts doesn't mean you should lose awareness of who you are, your core being and your values. Not recognizing and acting on your values will make you easily moved by the unrealistic and incomprehensible standards the critic wants you to live by.

To recognize your values, you have to examine yourself carefully, separating your true needs and beliefs from those of your peers, parents, society or spouse. Those unrealistic standards formed through the years of hearing your parents telling you the right way to behave should give way for your own values. While you are driven to meet those inflexible high standards out of self-doubt and shame, the desire to live a meaningful life pushes you to maintain your values.

Now is the time to practice the exercise that will help you recognize your true values.

**Exercise**

Hold up various areas of life and write down what you want and why you want what you want from each one of them –what are your core values about each of them. Also note down the level of importance you ascribe to each one of them. You can start by examining the following spheres of life, feel free to add yours:

1.  Physical self-care and health: write down the kinds of preventive changes, beauty routine, exercise or diet that you want to see in your life. Why do you want them? Are they very important to you, somewhat important or not so important? What are your values about physical self-care and health? If, for instance, your values include a brighter skin, strength or vitality, write them down.

2.  Family of origin: How important are your parents and siblings to you? Do you want to feel closer to them? Love them or be accepted by them?

3.  Parenting: When it comes to parenting, what is it that is important to you? Loving, protecting or providing for your kids?

4.  Intimate Relationships: What is your ideal relationship with your partner, friends, husband, wife or lover? Open? Loving? Warm? Based on wealth?

5.  Spirituality: What kind of spirituality do you want to have in your life? Spirituality takes different

forms. You may want to have a closer relationship with nature, a god or a higher power.

6.  Social life: What do you value about making new friends or having a social life? The love and trust that could come with it? The outdoor life? The social media pictures? Rank the importance of having a social life to you.

7.  Education: Why do you want to go to school or learn? Is it for the sake of gaining more wisdom or improving yourself?

8.  Career: Our careers usually take central place in our lives as we tend to spend a huge chunk of our lives at work. Ask yourself what you want to achieve in your career as well as the kind of work you find meaningful or suitable to your personality.

9.  Community Life: Do you seek to be charitable, just or an active part of your community life? Write it down. Also note down why you think it is important that you are all of those things.

10. Recreation and Leisure: how will you like to spend your leisure time? Engaging in exciting activities or bonding with your loved ones?

As you carry out this exercise, you will come to realize what's truly important and what you could stop bothering yourself about. You will stop wanting to be like every other person. The feelings of guilt or self-doubt will reduce because now that you are acting on your own values, you are no longer trying to please everybody. Truth is, there is no way you can ever please everybody and trying to do so will always do a number on your emotions.

Now that you've discovered what your true values are, strive to remember and be aware of them. Also ensure that you act on maintaining them every single day.

## A Better Way of Handling Mistakes

Now that you are aware of your core values, it is time to reframe the way you see mistakes. Mistakes are bound to happen, no matter how aware you are of your core values. However, the mistakes on their own have no power to upset your mental balance or water down the progress you've made so far in building a healthy self-esteem, it is your rationalization of these mistakes that have devastating effects on your self-esteem.

Trying to live your life by the high, incomprehensible or unrealistic standards of your parents or society is one of the reasons why you feel the way you do about mistakes. If you've always heard that you should not spend so much money on beauty products as they are vanity. You will find yourself feeling bad and regretting the few times you went against that rule and trying your best to avoid making such 'mistake' again.

You believe your critic when it tells you that the mistakes you've made is a proof of how worthless you are. But the truth is, mistakes are inevitable, and you can't be perfect at all times—which is okay. You need to consciously work on how you view mistakes.

The best way to handle mistakes is to start seeing them as:

> 1. A learning process: stop going over your past mistakes and beating yourself up about them, telling yourself that you should have done better. You know better now and you most likely won't repeat such again. If you had the knowledge you have now, you probably wouldn't have acted that way in the first place.

> Don't stop yourself from being spontaneous or trying new things because you fear failing or making a mistake. Your mindset should be "if I get it wrong, I'll at least learn the right way to do it next time."

> 2. A natural part of your life: No one in life is perfect and that is natural. Feel free to express your thoughts and do what you want to. If your words or actions disappoint someone or make you feel awkward. Remember that you cannot always be perfect –you can either learn from the mistakes or move on.

## Coping With Criticism

Just as you can't stop mistakes from occurring, you can't also stop people from criticizing you. Like mistakes, criticisms will influence your self-esteem only if you let them. Don't allow criticisms make you forget your self-esteem or core values.

To prevent criticism from having a damaging impact on your self-esteem, you have to learn how to cope with it. This segment will teach you how to respond to critics in an effective manner. But before that, there are a number of things you should understand about reality, they include the following:

1.  People are different: they see things differently, have different tastes, beliefs, behavior patterns and psychological makeup. You shouldn't regard their critical statements as the complete truth. For instance, someone who is naturally outgoing won't understand why you don't mingle with people. The person will immediately criticize you for being boring or too shy because he/she is unable to understand that your introverted is okay.

2.  Emotions color people's perceptions: When people are feeling a certain kind of way, their emotions often color their words or actions. Your boyfriend may have called you wasteful for using up the remaining oil because he just got fired from his job and is feeling paranoid. If you start going over his criticism in your head and believing that you lack judgment, your self-esteem suffers for something that is not even the truth.

In conclusion, before you accept any critical remark as the ultimate truth about yourself, first of all reflect on the critic's overall makeup or emotions.

And when responding to criticism, be neither passive nor aggressive, rather acknowledge the criticism by telling the person that they are right and provide explanation if necessary. That is the only way to stop criticism instantly.

## Practicing Assertiveness

Rejecting your core being and not being aware of your values keep you ignorant of your wants and needs. Not accepting yourself makes you feel your needs are not valid and not recognizing your values makes you clueless about what you want or need. And when you go around giving people what they want without acknowledging and asking for what you want, you will continue to feel less than everyone in the room and that will make you unhappy.

You have to take stock of your basic needs and whatever else you may want, and practice putting those needs or wants into words. Be direct, specific and clear when asking for what you want. Don't say "you need to change your attitude. Say instead, "I don't like how you keep spending recklessly." Or mention their name and state exactly what you want from them: "Nick, you keep teasing me in front of Victor, Jane and John, your siblings and I want you to stop doing that." When making your assertive requests, ensure that the facts are clear and straightforward.

Body language is also very important when you are making these requests. To work on your body language, you can stand in front of a mirror and practice making your requests. Standing close enough, maintaining eye contact and sitting or standing erect are all very necessary for driving in your message.

Don't use accusatory or judgmental words when making your request and be conscious of the tone of your voice—aim for moderation.

# CHAPTER 6
## BEING AND FEELING VALUED

Although the valuableness of your self-worth doesn't rely on external factors like your achievements or appearance, engaging in activities that you and many others find valuable can make your already perfect core shine even more brightly. Growing is a normal part of human lives. When you feel like you are not making progress in life, feelings of depression can easily set in.

You desire growth because deep down, you know that you can be even more. You can be more loving, intelligent, wise, smart, skillful and so on. Growing basically means developing the traits or capabilities that already exist in your core—being even more of what you already are. When you know that you are being the best person you can be at a pace that is suitable for you, you feel happy about yourself deep down.

Embracing and developing your core capabilities like the ability to love, show kindness, laugh, look amazing and so on strengthens your self-worth. You also make it easy for people to love you and want to be around you, further increasing your sense of self-worth.

While love should come naturally from your parents regardless of what you do, you will make it easier to receive love from your parents as well as others that matter to you when you act in ways that invite effortlessly invite love. Knowing that you are valued makes you feel valued and more accepting of yourself. This is why you should never stop developing your potentials and capacities, elevating humanity and moving towards excellence.

## Your self-worth could use a bit of help

Building your self-esteem through the belief that your core being is already perfect doesn't mean you should become complacent. Remember, you give the critic ammunition to attack you when you engage in actions that doesn't align with your core values. Silencing the critic becomes impossible when your actions overshadow rather than brighten your self-worth. Of course, you will believe the critic when it tells you that you are a bad or a hateful person if you use drugs in a way that harms your health or use derogatory words to describe other people.

Don't be misled by the idea of self-acceptance. To aid the process of personal development and growth, you need to accept yourself and allow your core being bloom like a flower at the same time. You can help your self-worth shine forth by doing the following:

- Eliminate behaviors that are not loving or self-promoting. This involves getting rid of any practices that are unkind or unhealthy like drug abuse, not getting enough sleep, eating disorderly, getting angry unnecessarily or objectifying sex.

- Learning new skills and staying conscious of the fact that you cannot be perfect.

- Expressing your feelings of gratitude, joy or satisfaction.

- Cultivating integrity and learning to appreciate the outside world like nature, art and beauty.

- Developing and nourishing your physical, emotional, spiritual, social and mental capacities.

The desire to develop ourselves stems from our innate desire to be happy. You find life exciting when you are happy with yourself.

## Achieving Your Goals

It is one thing to set goals but quite another thing to achieve those goals. You may have the strong desire to quit abusing drugs for instance, learn a new skill or become compassionate but discover that those desires of yours never become a reality. And you will feel dissatisfied, helpless and unhappy about it because it is the natural inclination to grow. Creating the kind of life, you want based on your core values strengthens your self-esteem.

Accepting yourself becomes easier for you when you are able to create changes and achieve your goals. As someone who is still struggling with poor self-esteem, you may keep finding reasons not to put in the amount of efforts required to achieve your goals. Reasons like lack of time, adequate information or believing that success is out of reach. You can overcome those stumbling blocks by doing the following:

1. Make adequate plan

You will get confused or overwhelmed by the steps you have to take to reach your goals if you dive straight into them without making sufficient plan. Achieving your goal become easier for you when you take your time to analyze and break down into bits, the steps that will help you arrive your goals. What are the skills, experience, resources or equipment that you will need and how can you get them? Answering questions like these will make better plan and prevent you from getting stuck, frustrated or confused halfway through achieving your goal.

2. Gather essential information

Of course, there is no way you can successfully achieve your goal if you lack the basic knowledge needed to do so. However, stop using this as an excuse when you can find the necessary information by simply searching for it. Sign up for a training, find a mentor, read books or carry out research on the internet.

3. Manage your time properly

Even if you gather essential information and make adequate plans, you will still be unable to achieve your goals if you never seem to have extra time on your hands. What activities do you engage in every day? Take stock of your daily activities and you may find yourself guilty of allowing tasks that are least important overshadow the important ones.

Learn to prioritize –taking care of the most important tasks first and the least important ones later. For instance, you could move painting your nails to the bottom of your to-do list and ascribe number 1 position to helping your kids with their homework. Creating a list of your daily tasks will help you know which one to do away with to make space for your goals.

Another thing you should learn is how to say no. Filter the requests based on their urgency or reasonability.

4. Imagine the worst

When you find yourself giving in to the fear of failure by not making any substantial effort to achieve your goal, ask yourself "what's the worst that could happen?" So, you get the job and get fired in a matter of weeks because they discover that you are a flop, or you summon the courage to go on stage and give a presentation but end up not making any sense. Okay, that's the worst that could happen, you don't know for sure how it will turn out until you try. Besides, what if you lose the job? You could get another job.

5. Stop trying to be perfect

You really should stop trying to be perfect. Remember that mistakes are inevitable, and they do not add to or take away your self-worth unless you let them. Do what you can at the moment, one step at a time. Hold on to your core values and don't give in to the pressure of living by other people's standards.

You can also apply the following techniques in addition to the above tips:

- **Visualize that you've already achieved your goals:** Practice visualizing the way you will look and act when you've achieved your goals. Create scenes in your mind in which you are in a satisfying relationship, no longer an alcoholic, learning how to code, have lost 50 pounds, more confident and doing whatever it is you want to.

The act of visualization reprograms the negative way you see yourself in your mind and causes you to act out what you already have in your subconscious. Believe it or not, visualization is a very effective tool you can use to bring yourself closer to achieving your dreams. Remember, poor self-esteem stems from seeing yourself as lesser than other human beings. It never crosses your mind for once that you are equal, so you keep choosing negative routes and negative people. Visualizing yourself differently can change all of that

**How do you practice visualization?** By simply finding a quiet spot that you can let yourself relax and simply breathe. Focus on breathing and playing the scenes you planned to visualize. Imagine yourself doing whatever you usually do every day—waking up, brushing your teeth and so on and then see yourself taking small, positive steps to achieve your goals. Definitely, distracting thoughts will come. The trick is to observe those thoughts without pursuing them and refocusing on the positive picture.

Practice visualization at least twice a day, once in the morning and at night before you sleep.

- **Have someone who will be checking up on you:** Another helpful technique is to share your short or long-term goals with a friend or family member and ask them to check up on you every week or so. Let the person know the steps you have to take to reach your goals as well as the timeframe that each step will demand.

You will be driven to stay committed to your goals as you will want to have a progressive report to give that friend or family member every week.

# CHAPTER 7
## ESSENTIAL FACTORS FOR MAINTAINING HEALTHY SELF-ESTEEM

This is like a recap of the previous chapters. Take this chapter as a quick pointer you can always visit when you find yourself forgetting the important factors necessary for building and maintaining healthy self-esteem. For easier reference, these factors are grouped into two major categories: perception and actions.

## Perception

Half of this workbook centers on changing and rebuilding the perception you have of yourself and the world at large. This requires becoming aware of and changing the way you view the following:

- **Core worth:** No matter what you do or don't do, your core worth remains perfect as a result of the inherent capabilities you were born with. However, developing these capabilities strengthens your core worth and makes it easier for you to accept yourself. Never stop taking steps, no matter how small, to develop your capabilities.

- **True values:** Recognizing your true values empowers you to break away from your critic's debasing hold. You become less prone to comparing yourself to others and feeling bad about not measuring up because you now understand who you are and why being different is okay. The guilt or feeling of worthlessness you experience when you don't meet up to your parents' or loved ones' standards dissipates because you are now driven to maintain your own values.

- **Mistakes:** See mistakes as an inevitable part of existence that has no influence on your self-worth. View them as a learning process and forgive yourself for past mistakes.

- **Thoughts:** Not every thought that flies into your mind is important. You can use the tips outlined in chapter 4 to distance yourself from your thoughts. See your thoughts as nothing more than mere thoughts that have nothing to do with who you really are. Practice meditation, thought labeling, forgiveness and acceptance.

- **Weakness:** The way you perceive your weaknesses can undermine your self-esteem or have no effect on it. Recognize your strengths and stop magnifying your weaknesses. Use the techniques provided in chapter 3 to reassess yourself and rewrite your weaknesses. Stop using pejorative, embellishing or generalizing words to describe yourself. And form a habit of celebrating yourself.

- **Criticism:** No matter the efforts you make to develop your capabilities, you will still find yourself at the receiving end of criticism. But these criticisms like mistakes will only be damaging to your self-worth if you let it. Stay conscious of the fact that people's perception of reality, beliefs, psychological makeup, background and current emotions affect what they say and do. Learn to respond to criticism in ways that are neither aggressive nor passive.

- **Perfection:** Saying that no one is perfect is easy but believing it is a whole different ballgame. But taking steps to change the way you see mistakes will prevent you from allowing the fear of failure stop you from pursuing your goals. Learn to love and accept those things you cannot change while making efforts to change those things you can. Once again, remember that your core being is already perfect.

## Actions

The other half of this workbook revolves around the active part of building and maintaining a healthy self-esteem. It requires you to do the following:

- Talk back at the critic: For each negative word your inner critic fires at you, shut it up with a blast of positive affirmations. Remember that your inner critic may have materialized from the unrealistic or vague rules and regulations set by your parents or caretakers or the devaluing words of your peers whose perception of reality was different from yours. Now that you have reassessed yourself and are aware of who you are, fight the critic with a string of positive words you now believe to be the truth.

- Be assertive: Stop ignoring your wants or needs. You will continue to see yourself as unimportant or undeserving of love and success if you keep doing so. Learn to ask for what you want in direct, clear and straightforward terms.

- Visualize your goals: Practice the visualization exercise outlined in chapter 6. Visualizing brings you a step closer to achieving your goals.

- Act on your values: Knowing your values and not acting on them can cause you a world of pain. There is no way you will feel happy or good about yourself if you keep relegating your values to the background in favor of other people's own. Take time to note down your values and go over them till they sink into your consciousness. Act on your values every day till they become a natural part of your existence.

- Express and share your capabilities: Every human is born with the capability of loving, showing kindness, laughing, forgiving and so on. Expressing and sharing these capabilities polishes your core worth and makes you feel better about yourself.

## Prepare for Setbacks

Even as you apply the skills you have learnt here both consciously and unconsciously, you may have moments when you'd feel like you are still not okay or not getting it right. It is important that you return to this book and review the self-esteem building skills once again.

Developing and maintaining one's self-esteem is an ongoing process—something you should keep repeating like you would any other important health practice. Once you have acquired self-esteem skills, applying them becomes easier with time.

However, when it comes to poor self-esteem, some people have it worse than others. These people would rather embrace unhealthy ways of avoiding the pain rather than face the pain head-on because they feel so vulnerable. If you are like this, you probably started feeling like something was wrong with you right from your earliest childhood.

Maybe you experienced physical or emotional abandonment as a child or constantly faced rejection from your peers. These experiences made you feel like you were at fault, like there was something basically wrong with you. Growing up, encountering any form of criticism, anger, rejection or even the mildest hurt, intensifies your feeling of worthlessness. Even when people actually compliment you or try to associate with you, you keep being scare that they will see through you one day.

This fear makes you constantly rage at yourself, others or seek refuge in emotional isolation, alcohol or drugs. You subconsciously think that attacking yourself is a way of atoning for your sins or that it will move you to sit up and do better.

People who feel this vulnerable are often too scared of the pain to abandon their coping mechanism and work on healthier ways of facing the pain. But all hope is not lost. You can stop allowing the immediacy of pain to fool you. It is thinking that you can't stand the pain or that the pain will last forever that pushes you to reach out for what you view as a faster escape route.

Change the way you think about the pain. Tell yourself that it won't last forever, that you are only feeling that way because of your early hurts and that the way you feel doesn't have any impact on your true worth. Sure, you may still find yourself struggling to believe those words but say them anyway.

The visualization technique can also come in very handy here. Allow yourself to breath and relax and them imagine that the pain has a specific shape or color. With each deep breath you take, see the pain moving farther away from you till it disappears. Turn a deaf ear to the negative thoughts that keep surfacing. Say to yourself "I will survive these old feelings that these kinds of situation are always triggering."

Thinking about your personal good times can also be resourceful. Search your memory for moments when you felt worthwhile or good about yourself and allow yourself to bask in the warm glow that those moments elicited in you. Make those positive memories or fantasies you have of yourself an anchor that you can hold on to when the negative feelings arise.

## Visit a Therapist

There is always the option of seeing a therapist if you still find it extremely difficult to get past the feeling of wrongness or worthlessness. The fact that you still feel bad about yourself even after trying the techniques in this book doesn't mean your situation is hopeless. It probably means that you are one out of thousands of people who needs the direct assistance of an experienced psychotherapist to overcome those persevering negative feelings.

Spending time with a therapist who sees exactly who you are and accepts your not-so-perfect qualities is capable of bringing about substantial changes over time—research has shown. Don't be scared to seek professional assistance.

# CONCLUSION

You have learned that the experiences you had in the past have a way of influencing the way you act or see yourself in the present. Your self-esteem is poor probably because you have been revisiting these painful past events and feeling bad about the way you were or thinking that you are a hopeless failure. But with the tools you have been armed with in this book, you can work at letting go of the painful memories of the past, accepting what you can't change and loving yourself regardless of it all.

Remember that having a healthy self-esteem is important as it is the only thing that will make you feel happy with yourself, worthy enough to be successful and capable of achieving your goals. Regardless of however you may feel in the process of building your self-esteem, keep at it. Consistency will definitely get you there!

www.ingramcontent.com/pod-product-compliance
Lightning Source LLC
La Vergne TN
LVHW090021180726
843489LV00008B/2920